T0011390

Ultimate Sticker Book
GARDEN FLOWERS

DK
Penguin Random House

With thanks to Ben Hoare for first edition text on pages 4–7 and 10–11

Project Editor Radhika Haswani
Senior Editor Dawn Sirett
US Senior Editor Shannon Beatty
Art Editor Bhagyashree Nayak
Designer Rachael Hare
Managing Editors Monica Saigal, Penny Smith
Managing Art Editor Ivy Sengupta
DTP Designers Dheeraj Singh, Nand Kishor Acharya
Picture Researchers Vagisha Pushp, Shubhdeep Kaur
Jacket Designer Rachael Hare
Jacket Coordinator Magda Pszuk
Production Editor Becky Fallowfield
Production Controller Leanne Burke
Delhi Creative Head Malavika Talukder
Deputy Art Director Mabel Chan
Publisher Francesca Young
Publishing Director Sarah Larter

Royal Horticultural Society
Consultant Helen Bostock; **Editor** Simon Maughan
Publisher Helen Griffin; **Head of Editorial** Tom Howard

This edition published in 2024
Previously published as
Ultimate Sticker Book: Garden Flowers (2006)
by DK Publishing
1745 Broadway, 20th Floor, New York, NY 10019
in association with The Royal Horticultural Society

FSC
MIX
Paper | Supporting responsible forestry
www.fsc.org   FSC™ C018179

This book was made with Forest Stewardship Council™ certified paper—one small step in DK's commitment to a sustainable future.
For more information go to www.dk.com/our-green-pledge

Activities

Here are the six different types of activities that you will find inside this book. Have fun!

Find it! Hunt for the correct stickers that fit the blank spaces.

Follow! Follow the trail and put the correct stickers on the pages.

Match it! Match the correct sticker with each picture to complete the images.

Make it! Put stickers on the pages to create your own scene.

Fit it! Find the stickers that fit the blank spaces and complete the big picture.

Guess it! Try the fun sticker quiz. All the answers are in the book!

Acknowledgments

The publisher would like to thank the following for their kind permission to reproduce their photographs:
(Key: a=above; b=below/bottom; c=center; f=far; l=left; r=right; t=top)

1 Dreamstime.com: Beata Becla (cra); Cynoclub (cla/X2); Le Thuy Do (cl); Sergey Kolesnikov (bl). **2–3 Dreamstime.com:** Greenfire (c); Paul Maguire (b). **2–13 Dreamstime.com:** Aga7ta (Pattern). **2 Alamy Stock Photo:** Miriam Heppell (cb). **Dreamstime.com:** Cynoclub (tr); Tetiana Zbrodko (c); Youths (cb/tools); James Phelps (bl). **3 Depositphotos Inc:** imagebrokermicrostock (r). **Dreamstime.com:** Kitchner Bain (bc); Slowmotiongli (crb). **Getty Images / iStock:** Nerthuz (cl). **4 Dreamstime.com:** Alexstar (br); X3mwoman (cr); Julia Sudnitskaya (bl). **Getty Images / iStock:** E+ / phototropic (bc). **4–5 Dreamstime.com:** KMNPhoto (t). **5 Dreamstime.com:** Le Thuy Do (tr, br). **Shutterstock.com:** Kisialiou Yury (bl). **6 Dreamstime.com:** Miroslav Hlavko (tl); Verastuchelova (tr); Yongsky (clb). **7 Dreamstime.com:** Grzegorz Kordus (tr); Iva Vagnerova (clb); Tom Meaker (crb). **Getty Images / iStock:** Magdevski (br). **8–9 Alamy Stock Photo:** WILDLIFE GmbH. **10 Shutterstock.com:** AlekseyKarpenko (cla). **11 Dreamstime.com:** Bruce Macqueen (tr). **12 Dreamstime.com:** Rob Lumen Captum (ca); Helgardas (br). **Getty Images / iStock:** akova (bl). **13 Alamy Stock Photo:** Jenny Lilly (tl). **Depositphotos Inc:** silver-bb (crb). **Dreamstime.com:** Liudmyla Ivashchenko (cb); Nailia Schwarz (clb). **Getty Images:** imageBROKER / Konrad Wothe (tr). **14–15 Getty Images / iStock:** elenaleonova. **16 Depositphotos Inc:** imagebrokermicrostock (tl). **Dreamstime.com:** Aga7ta (Pattern); Alexander Chicherin (cla); Anastasiia Malinich (cb); Agenturfotografin (crb); Alfio Scisetti (cb/berries); Tom Meaker (tr); Julia Sudnitskaya (fbl); Yongsky (cra); Nailia Schwarz (br). **Getty Images / iStock:** E+ / phototropic (bl). **Shutterstock.com:** Kisialiou Yury (ca). **18 Depositphotos Inc:** imagebrokermicrostock (cla). **Dreamstime.com:** Agenturfotografin (tl); Tetiana Zbrodko (tc/hydrangea); Greenfire (tl/fence); Cynoclub (butterflyX14); Sandra Van Der Steen (tr); Paul Maguire (Grass BG); Roman Samokhin (clb); Tamara Kulikova (crb); James Phelps (cra); Aleksandar Grozdanovski (ca, b/SnailX4); Justforever (cb). **19 Dreamstime.com:** Alexstar (cl, bl/X6); Le Thuy Do (tc, cr); KMNPhoto (tr); X3mwoman (ca); Julia Sudnitskaya (c, clb/X6). **Shutterstock.com:** Kisialiou Yury (tl/br). **22 Dreamstime.com:** Miroslav Hlavko (tl, fclb/X2); Yongsky (tc/Cyclamen, fcrb/X2); Verastuchelova (tc, clb/X2); Grzegorz Kordus (tr, crb/X2); Tom Meaker (cla/br); Iva Vagnerova (ca, crb/X4). **Getty Images / iStock:** Magdevski (cra, clb/X4). **23 Alamy Stock Photo:** WILDLIFE GmbH (RoseX9). **Dreamstime.com:** Alexander Chicherin (tr); Moskwa (c, br/X4). **26 Alamy Stock Photo:** Jenny Lilly (fclb/X2). **Dreamstime.com:** Alexander Chicherin (fclb/X2); X3mwoman (clb/X2); Anastasiia Malinich (tl); Valentyn75 (cla, cb/X4); Richard Griffin (tr, crb/X4); Sergey Kolesnikov (ca, clb/X4); Alfio Scisetti (cra, bc/X4). **Getty Images:** imageBROKER / Konrad Wothe (cl). **27 Alamy Stock Photo:** Ernie Janes (crb, bl/X2); Jenny Lilly (cb). **Depositphotos Inc:** silver-bb (cra, br/X2). **Dreamstime.com:** Rob Lumen Captum (clb); Liudmyla Ivashchenko (tl); Nailia Schwarz (tc); Helgardas (ca). **Getty Images / iStock:** akova (tr). **Getty Images:** imageBROKER / Konrad Wothe (cl). **30 Depositphotos Inc:** miltonia (br). **Dreamstime.com:** Alekss (crb); Sandra Van Der Steen (tl); Nerthuz (tr); Olena Vasylieva (ca/gloves); Gustavo Andrade (tr/snail); Nynke Van Holten (clb); Jakub Krechowicz (cl); Justforever (c); William Berry (cr); Postnikov (clb/boots); Atman (cb/Rake); Vbmark (crb/fbl); Aquariagirl1970 (bl); Povarov (bc); Domnitsky (cl/worms). **31 Alamy Stock Photo:** Ernie Janes (cr/X3). **Depositphotos Inc:** silver-bb (cra/X3). **Dreamstime.com:** Alekss (crb/ladybugsX2); Alexstar (br); X3mwoman (c/X3); Yongsky (bl/X3); Verastuchelova (ca/X3); Grzegorz Kordus (bc/X3); Alexander Chicherin (clb/X3); Sergey Kolesnikov (crb/X2); Sandra Van Der Steen (clb/X2); William Berry (cb/X2); Postnikov (clb/bootsX2); Atman (cb/RakeX2); Vbmark (cb/butterflyX2); Aquariagirl1970 (cb/spadeX2); Moskwa (clb/X3); Richard Griffin (cb/DaisyX2); Julia Sudnitskaya (cl)

Cover images: Front: 123RF.com: antonel (daisyx2); **Alamy Stock Photo:** Ernie Janes clb; **Dreamstime.com:** Richard Griffin bc, Liudmyla Ivashchenko ca, Tom Meaker cra, Nailia Schwarz cla, Alfio Scisetti / Scisettialfio tr, Liubov Shirokova br; **Getty Images / iStock:** ranasu tl, ftr; **Shutterstock.com:** Kisialiou Yury crb; **Back: 123RF.com:** antonel br, Roman Samokhin / usersam2007 bl; **Dreamstime.com:** Fibobjects (Daisyx2), Alfio Scisetti / Scisettialfio tr, Liubov Shirokova fbr; **Getty Images / iStock:** ranasu tc

All other images © Dorling Kindersley

In the garden

Amazing flowering plants can be grown in spaces that are big or small, shady or sunny, wet and boggy, or windswept and dry. Let's learn more about beautiful gardens!

Earthworm

Bugs and creepy-crawlies

Bugs and creepy-crawlies love gardens that are full of plants. Butterflies and bees feed on flower nectar. Bees eat the flower pollen, too, while snails chomp on leaves and other parts of plants. And earthworms eat the decaying plants within the soil.

Bee

Flowers

Flowers such as pansies, poppies, and hydrangeas add bright colors to gardens. Flowers can also smell lovely, and they attract butterflies, ladybugs, bees, and other bugs.

Butterfly

Poppies

Ladybug

Hydrangeas

Pansies

Watering can

Wheelbarrow

Rake

Pots

Shovel

Equipment and tools

Equipment such as a watering can is useful in any garden, and a wheelbarrow is helpful in a larger space. Garden tools such as shovels, forks, and rakes are used for preparing and digging the soil and making it ready for new plants and seeds.

Sunlight

Plants need the sun's energy to grow. They use sunlight, air, and water to make their own food.

Trees

Trees come in many shapes and sizes. Small fruit trees are a good choice for a small yard. Fruit trees such as cherry and apple trees have beautiful flower blossoms that usually appear in spring.

Apple tree

Bird

Snail

Daffodils

Soil

A plant's roots are anchored in soil. This keeps the plant secure as it grows. Soil also stores water and nutrients that plants need.

Sun-loving flowers

Some garden flowers need plenty of sun and won't grow as well if they're hidden away in dark corners. These sun-lovers thrive in hot and dry areas.

Geranium

These flowers are usually red, pink, peach, white, or purple. They are easy to grow. People often put them in window boxes and hanging baskets.

Sunflower

Sunflowers are easy to grow from seeds. Some varieties can reach heights of up to 12 ft (3.5 m) in just six months.

Iris

These tall-stemmed flowers come in lots of different colors. They are named after Iris, the Greek goddess of rainbows.

Magnolia

Magnolias are pretty trees with showy flowers. The flowers appear in spring or summer and may be cream, pink, or deep red in color.

Clematis

A clematis grows quickly up walls, tree trunks, and along hedges. As the plant climbs, its leaf stalks curl around anything they can find for support.

The tulip is the national flower of Turkey, Iran, and the Netherlands.

Dahlia

Dahlias come in many shapes and colors. Some dahlia flowers can be as big as dinner plates!

Tulip

Brightly colored tulips grow from bulbs, which need to be planted in the fall. The bulbs produce flowers the next spring.

Snowdrop

The snowdrop has bell-like flowers that are as white as snow. This tough little plant blooms in winter even when the soil is frozen or covered in snow.

Foxglove

This tall plant grows in the woods, and has pink or purple flowers in summer. Many parts of the foxglove plant are poisonous.

Cyclamen

This pretty little plant blooms in autumn, winter, and spring. It grows from a thickened underground stem called a tuber, and can survive cold, wintry weather. Cyclamen flowers can be white, pink, or red.

Match it!

Shade-loving flowers

The flowers on these pages will all tolerate growing in shady places, such as under a tree or in the shadow of a house. They usually don't mind a little sun, and do best in soil that is kept moist.

Fuchsia

A fuchsia's flowers are long, droopy, and tube-shaped. They are mostly multicolored and look perfect in hanging baskets.

Lily of the valley

This plant bears small, white, bell-shaped flowers in spring. It has a wonderful fragrance and was traditionally used in wedding posies.

Daffodil

The cheerful daffodil grows wild in woods and hedges, and it thrives in gardens, too. The bulbs should be planted in large groups for a more dramatic effect.

Bluebell

It is best to plant bluebell bulbs in groups under trees or bushes. They burst into flower in spring, creating a carpet of blue blooms.

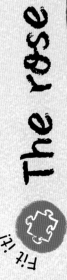

The rose

Roses are beautiful and often fragrant, and some varieties keep flowering from spring until autumn, providing gorgeous blooms for many months. Known as the queen of flowers, the rose comes in many colors—red, pink, yellow, white, orange, and purple. It is a very popular garden plant.

You can buy rose water (made from soaking rose petals in water), as well as rose petal powder, both of which are said to soothe, strengthen, and heal the skin.

Some roses have many layers of petals. Flowers like this are called double flowers.

Nearly all roses prefer a sunny spot, but some will grow in shady places.

Rosa John Keats (a shrub or climbing rose)

Green, leaflike sepals protect the young flower buds.

Types of roses

Roses can be found growing in many different parts of the world, in any place that suits them. There are about 150 species of the rose plant growing in the wild, and gardeners can choose from thousands of rose varieties. These varieties are grouped into types, such as hybrid tea roses and climbing roses. Each rose type has different characteristics.

Hybrid tea roses

This type of rose is common in gardens. It usually has one flower on each stem, rather than clusters of flowers.

Climbing roses

Climbing roses have large single or clustered flowers. They grow over walls, arches, and fences.

As well as being used in skin products, rose petals are used to make perfumes and herbal teas.

9

Plants for wildlife

Gardens are a haven for wildlife. Flower nectar, berries, and seedheads are a source of food for many garden creatures. Help this bird find the way to its nest as it visits garden flowers and finds food along the way.

Sparrow

START

Wild aster

Birdbath

Stop for a bath!

Cotoneaster

Calendula

Tasty seeds!

Ground feeder

Crunchy peanuts!

Bird feeder

Watch out!

Pet cat

Guelder rose

Coneflower

FINISH

Helpful flowers

Reward yourself with a flower sticker every time you visit a flower that provides food for wildlife.

Guelder rose

In the fall, birds love to eat this plant's bright red berries.

Calendula

This marigold has open flowers, which attract hoverflies and bees. Its seedheads provide food for birds.

Cotoneaster

Many birds love cotoneaster berries. This plant produces creamy white flowers.

Wild aster

This flower looks great planted in flowerbeds or pots. Insects visit its blooms for nectar and pollen. Birds like to feast on its seedheads.

Coneflower

The coneflower's petals point out and downward. Its prickly seedheads attract birds and butterflies.

Fascinating flowers

There are so many different types of flowers. Let's take a look at some wonderfully eye-catching blooms! Which one do you like the best?

Amethyst in snow

This flower has silky, tube-shaped, white and purple fringed petals. It is beautiful to look at and attracts lots of bugs.

Blue poppy

Flowers that are bright blue like these blue poppies are a rare sight. The yellow centers of these flowers are rich in pollen—perfect for bumblebees.

Bearded iris

These fragrant flowers are named after the fuzzy "beard" on their downward-facing petals. They have tall stems and swordlike leaves.

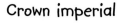

Crown imperial

The tall crown imperial has large, striking, bell-shaped flowers that are covered in a crown of green leaves. Its flowers come in shades of orange, yellow, and red.

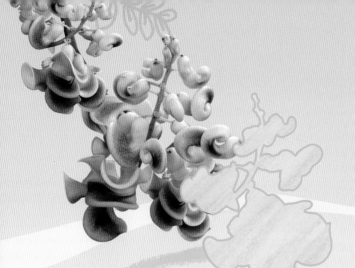

Lady's slipper orchid

These unique-looking orchids have a slipper-like pouch shape. They are also unusual in that they don't produce nectar.

Snail vine

This easy-to-grow, tropical climbing plant gets its name from its flower buds that have a spiral shape like a snail's shell. Its flowers are purple and white, and very fragrant.

Passion flower

Passion flowers climb and grow over other plants. The exotic-looking blooms of this plant have pointed petals and delicate fringed petals that attract butterflies and bees.

Snake's head fritillary

This bell-shaped, nodding flower has a unique checkered pattern, and is said to look like a scaly snake's head—hence the plant's name. The flowers can be purple, pink, or white.

Bleeding heart

This plant has wonderful, pink, heart-shaped flowers that hang from long stems. Bleeding heart plants contain a substance that is harmful to people and pets when eaten or touched.

Make it! Create your own garden

What would you like to grow in this garden? You could add some stickers of flowers, such as roses, dahlias, and daffodils. You could also stick on a few butterflies and creepy-crawlies, as well as some garden tools and equipment.

Guess it!

Sticker quiz

Reward yourself with a flower sticker for each question you answer correctly.

1. In which season do flower blossoms usually appear on cherry and apple trees?

2. Which bulb flowers grow in the woods in spring and create a carpet of blue blooms?

3. Which flower is known as the queen of flowers?

4. What is the national flower of Turkey, Iran, and the Netherlands?

5. Which flower has a crown of green leaves?

6. What is the name of the thickened underground stem that plants such as cyclamens grow from?

7. Name two garden plants that provide berries for birds.

8. Name these colorful garden flowers.

9. Which flower is named after the Greek goddess of rainbows?

10. Which flower has a unique checkered pattern, and is said to look like a reptile's head?

1. Spring 2. Bluebell 3. Rose 4. Tulip 5. Crown imperial 6. Tuber 7. Cotoneaster and guelder rose 8. Pansies 9. Iris 10. Snake's head fritillary